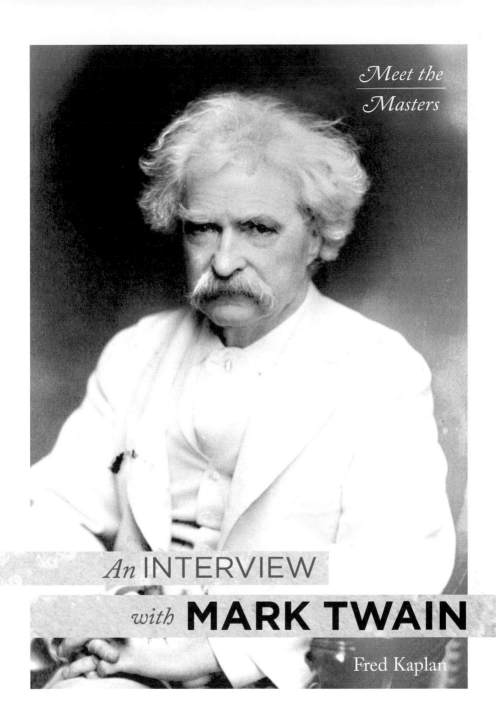

Meet the
Masters

An INTERVIEW

with **MARK TWAIN**

Fred Kaplan

Cavendish
Square

New York

Published in 2015 by Cavendish Square Publishing, LLC
243 5th Avenue, Suite 136, New York, NY 10016

CPSIA Compliance Information: Batch #WS14CSQ

All websites were available and accurate when this book was sent to press.

Library of Congress Cataloging-in-Publication Data

Kaplan, Fred, 1937-
An interview with Mark Twain / Fred Kaplan.
pages cm. — (Meet the masters)
Includes index.
ISBN 978-1-62712-900-8 (hardcover) ISBN 978-1-62712-902-2 (ebook)
1. Twain, Mark, 1835-1910. I. Title.
PS1331.K315 2014
818'.409—dc23
[B]
2014002803

Editorial Director: Dean Miller   Designer: Amy Greenan
Senior Editor: Fletcher Doyle   Production Manager: Jennifer Ryder-Talbot
Senior Copy Editor: Wendy A. Reynolds   Production Editor: David McNamara
Art Director: Jeffrey Talbot   Photo Research: J8 Media

CONTENTS

In Twain's novel, Huck Finn felt wicked for bucking social convention by following his own sense of what's right and helping Jim.

FOREWORD

by Jay McInerney

Humor is notoriously **evanescent**—with a shelf life somewhere between that of a fish and a software program—and yet, almost a hundred years after his death, Mark Twain remains one of the most durable and popular American writers. *The 2007 Yale Book of Quotations* has 153 quotations from Twain—140 more than Karl Marx. Many of Twain's "serious" and high-minded contemporaries, such as his friend William Dean Howells, are little more than footnotes to literary history while Twain continues to acquire new readers: when my son was twelve he picked up and finished *Tom Sawyer* of his own volition, without prompting from myself, his mother, or a teacher.

"It was cool," was his **laconic** assessment.

Twain grew up on the banks of the Mississippi and served as a riverboat pilot in his early twenties. When he was twenty-five, he went West to seek his fortune. Much of his greatest comedy derives from skewering the gullible optimism and exuberant greed of the young republic. He found rich fodder in the great American belief in the big score, the lucky strike, the pot of gold at the end of the rainbow—a tendency that he thoroughly embodied in his own life. No matter how much money Twain made from his writing, he was always involved in get-rich schemes, and lost several fortunes in mining stocks, bogus inventions, and dubious business ventures.

Smarter in his work than in his life, he almost never condescended to his characters, no matter how foolish or venal. Twain shuttles effortlessly between the ostensibly distant poles of sheer antic nonsense and sermonizing. "The Celebrated Jumping Frog of Calaveras County" (1865) is pure fluff, a tall tale that does nothing more than send up the art of tall-tale telling and the rough manners and colorful speech of the Western mining camps where Twain spent time in his twenties.

"A True Story, Repeated Word for Word as I Heard It" (1874) is an indictment not only of slavery but of the stupidity of the narrator himself (presumably Twain) for imagining that the life of an ol' black mammy was idyllic. Both of these stories, like most of Twain's work, were told in an American **vernacular** which helped to forge an idiomatic American literary tradition thoroughly distinct from European antecedents.

When Mark Twain decided to let Tom Sawyer's scruffy buddy Huck tell his own story, he unleashed one of the great comic voices of American literature and discovered a finely tuned instrument of social critique: among the great ironies that energize the novel is the fact that Huck, the social outcast, feels guilty for transgressing the most unjust and artificial of contemporary social conventions. Huck confuses convention with natural law just as he confuses his own innate sense of morality with "wickedness" when he imagines that he's going to Hell for helping Jim, the runaway slave who becomes his companion.

Floating down the Mississippi on their raft, Huck and Jim enact the great American fantasy of escaping civilization for the wide open spaces even as they stumble upon a dizzying cross-section of society. Few novels have so thoroughly embodied the promises and contradictions of the American character; none comes close to doing so with such exuberance and such a high quotient of sheer entertainment. Most classics inevitably carry the whiff of the classroom; reading Twain feels like playing hookey.

INTRODUCTION

A master of **repartee** and never too busy to respond to a request for an interview, Mark Twain set the gold standard for verbal wit and self-revelation in his writings and public statements. In this book he makes a postmortem appearance, as usual with a cigar in his hand and dressed in an immaculate white suit. An obsessive self-dramatist, he reveled in his own striking presence. He was a master of the interview form, and always answered the question he wanted to answer, which was not necessarily the question he was asked.

During a life that spanned two-thirds of the nineteenth century, he was often depicted in drawings and photographs. Widely appreciated for his evocation of American culture, his caustic wit, and his satiric vision, he was instantly recognizable by the newspaper-reading as well as the book-reading public. By old age, he had become an American icon.

Mark Twain honed his verbal skills in impromptu exchanges with reporters and on his lecture tours, in which he entertained audiences with oral performances of edited selections from his books.

Samuel Langhorne Clemens told several versions of how he picked up the pseudonym Mark Twain.

To Twain, writing was closely related to talking. In both his authorial and his speaking voice he emphasized a colloquial, conversational directness and simplicity that made him a friendly, folksy, and companionable voice. He was never at a loss for words. His prodigious memory provided him with an instantly available anthology of the best of what he had written. His talent for spontaneous as well as well-honed witty **maxims** and general observations made him an interviewer's delight. During the last decades of his life, he wrote extensive reminiscences and comments on contemporary life into notebooks which he called his "autobiography." They are another form of speech, as if he is talking both to himself and to us.

Meet the Masters: An Interview with Mark Twain is intended to be more conversation in this tradition, another instance of the master of self-revelation creating and commenting on himself and his culture. Always adept at self-advertisement, he had both the talent and the incentive to master the interview form. He was his own best publicist and did not distinguish between selling himself and selling his books: It was a single process. Because he specialized in being eminently quotable, some of his published words are incorporated into his responses in this latest encounter. Echoing the style of his published interviews, comments, and autobiographical meanderings, here once again is the distinctive voice of a unique American writer.

1

MARK TWAIN: HIS LIFE IN SHORT

Born in Florida, Missouri, on November 30, 1835, Samuel Langhorne Clemens was the sixth child of a failed lawyer and merchant, John M. Clemens, born in 1798, and of Jane Lampton Clemens, born in 1803, the daughter of Benjamin Lampton of Kentucky. They married in 1823 in Kentucky and moved to Tennessee, where John purchased land and opened a law practice. In 1839, the family moved to Hannibal, Missouri, on the Mississippi River, where Samuel Clemens—Mark Twain, as we know him—spent his early years. His father died when he was twelve. His respected and adored mother lived until 1890.

Twain was a precocious child. In his autobiographical writings (not always factually reliable) and in the recollections of his contemporaries he is depicted as a free-thinking and mischievous boy who questioned many of the conventions and beliefs of his Protestant frontier society. A rapidly developing small city in a slave state, Hannibal became the fictional St. Petersburg in *The Adventures of Huckleberry Finn* (1884) and *Pudd'nhead Wilson* (1894). Twain's formal education was restricted to Sunday and grade schools. At twelve years of age he began work as an **apprentice** printer.

By 1853, the Clemens family had left Hannibal—Twain's mother and sister for St. Louis, and Twain for New York and Philadelphia, where he worked as a printer. He soon returned

In 1874, Mark Twain and his wife Olivia moved into this house in Hartford, Connecticut.

Samuel Clemens, holding a printer's composing stick with letters spelling out his name, worked as a printer at the age of fifteen.

to the Midwest, where in 1857 he fulfilled a boyhood fantasy—qualifying to become an apprentice riverboat pilot on the Mississippi, after getting only as far as New Orleans in his plan to find riches in South America.

An avid **autodidact** who read extensively from an early age, Twain would also emphasize how central his pre-authorial work experiences were to his education as a writer. Though he later reminisced about his riverboat pilot years as the best of his life, he admitted in *Life on the Mississippi* (1883) his difficulty in mastering the river and how much he feared causing a shipwreck. Eventually he qualified as a licensed pilot. In early 1861, when Union gunboats closed the river, he hid at his sister's home in St. Louis, avoiding both Confederate and Union **conscription**. He served briefly as a Confederate militia volunteer near Hannibal, and then went to Nevada as an assistant to his brother Orion, whom the Lincoln government had appointed secretary of the territory. After a frustrating year mining for silver and gold, in September 1862 he became a reporter for the *Virginia City Territorial Enterprise* under the byline "Mark Twain." This was his first appearance as a professional writer.

Between 1863 and 1866, Twain divided his time between Virginia City and San Francisco, writing also for San Francisco newspapers and publishing sketches in East Coast magazines. In summer 1866, he sailed to Hawaii as a travel correspondent and then published twenty letters from Hawaii in the *Alta California*, which he later incorporated into his second travel book, *Roughing It* (1872). In autumn 1866, he gave his first public lecture, a humorous account of his Hawaiian Island experiences. The following year he sailed from New York on the *Quaker City*, employed by the *Alta California* to provide travel letters about the much-publicized voyage of this steamer to Palestine. The letters were revised into his first and most successful travel book, *The Innocents Abroad* (1869). In the meantime, his book of humorous sketches, *The Celebrated Jumping Frog of Calaveras County* (1865), had been published.

Mark Twain wrote *The Adventures of Huckleberry Finn* in this pilot house-shaped cottage in his wife's hometown of Elmira.

With Elisha Bliss, his publisher in Hartford, Connecticut, Twain cooperated in marketing his books, usually lavishly illustrated, and sold by prepaid subscription by traveling salesmen to the mostly rural public to whom he appealed as a humorist. His aspiration to be seen as a serious writer, an intellectually sharp satirist as well as a popular author, increased after his marriage in 1870 to the well-educated and well-to-do Olivia Langdon of Elmira, New York, whom he met through her brother, who had also sailed on the *Quaker City*.

Twain supplemented his income as a newspaper writer and humorist with extensive and exhausting lecture tours in 1869 and 1870, consisting of readings from his humorous works. He would continue to undertake lecture tours irregularly until the mid-1880s. The Langdon family welcomed and generously supported the marriage, with the wedding gift of a house in Buffalo and the purchase of part-ownership for Twain in the *Buffalo Express*.

In 1871, disenchanted with Buffalo and concerned about a sickly infant son (who would die in 1872), Twain moved to Hartford, where Livy gave birth to Susy in 1872, Clara in 1874, and Jean in 1880. The elaborate house that Twain had built in the Nook Farm area became the center of his hospitality and friendships; distinguished writers, editors, and politicians were his neighbors, including Harriet Beecher Stowe. With his Hartford friends he founded the Saturday Morning Club for young ladies and joined the Monday Evening Club for intellectual discussion.

A regular visitor to Boston and New York for professional engagements and general entertainment, Twain counted among his close literary friends William Dean Howells and Bret Harte; with the latter he collaborated on a number of plays before the friendship collapsed. Attracted to the theater for its glamor and financial prospects, Twain never managed, despite many efforts, to master the theatrical formulas for the kind of popular success he desired.

Now a world-famous writer, his reputation was solidified by his visits to Great Britain in 1872–1873, where he gave lectures, and to Germany, Switzerland, and France in 1878–1879, the latter forming the basis for his third travel book, *A Tramp Abroad* (1880). In 1873, he coauthored, with his neighbor and friend Charles Dudley Warner, *The Gilded Age: A Tale of Today*, a widely discussed novel that gave its name to the post-Civil War era of corruption and affluence. Twain's popularity and his literary reputation reached their **apogee** during his lifetime in the 1880s with the publication of *The Prince and the Pauper* (1881), *Life on the Mississippi*, and *Huckleberry Finn*.

With a handsome income from writing and his wife's inheritance, Twain took the opportunity, beginning in the mid-1870s, to pursue his passion for technological innovation and financial **speculation**. In 1877, he had one of the first telephone lines in Hartford established in his home. Earlier he had tried his commercial luck with two inventions of his own, a self-pasting scrapbook and an improved type of suspenders.

Investing in 1880 in a new process for making engraved printing plates, he lost about $50,000 in nineteenth century dollars (or about a million present-day dollars) on the project. Between 1886 and 1895 he lost the modern equivalent of at least $10 million in his backing of the failed Paige Compositor, a typesetter that he expected would become the standard for printing newspapers and books. In the mid-1880s, dissatisfied with the sales of his books by a succession of publishers, he formed his own publishing company under the name of his business manager, his nephew by marriage, C.L. Webster, which brought out *Huckleberry Finn*. When the company failed, the **vitriolic** Twain, who lost most of his investment, blamed his partner.

On the one hand, the 1880s brought him international literary fame and respect; on the other, his speculations and financial losses brought him anxiety, insecurity, and restlessness, aggravating the long-standing tension between his need for security and his attraction to risk-taking. His literary efforts increasingly reflected both elements. He produced a series of literary works created almost exclusively to make money, such as his play *Colonel Sellers* (1886) and *Mark Twain's Library of Humor* (1888). He also published acerbic satirical attacks on human fallibility and the mismanagement of social and political organizations that had little or no chance of selling well, particularly *A Connecticut Yankee in King Arthur's Court* (1889) and *Pudd'nhead Wilson.* These reflect the large number of similar harsh critiques of people and society that the realistic and disenchanted Twain wrote but rarely published, starting with characters *Huck Finn and Tom Sawyer Among the Indians* in 1884 and culminating with what are known as the *Mysterious Stranger Manuscripts* (1897–1904) and the privately printed *What Is Man?* (1906).

His precarious financial ice skating and his jaded view of human nature did not prevent Twain from continuing to be a devoted husband and father. A sentimental Victorian in this regard, he idolized his wife and idealized domestic life. His 1895 novel *Personal Recollections of Joan of Arc*, whom he regarded as an embodiment of perfect womanhood, contained something of Twain's view of his wife. Livy's love of German culture and language and their mutual desire to provide a private continental European education for their daughters contributed to their decision to reside in Germany and Italy in 1891–1892. But it was Twain's financial setbacks that weighed most heavily in the decision to leave their beloved but expensive Hartford life. With Twain making frequent business trips back to the United States, they continued to live abroad, mostly because of the delusion that they could live more cheaply in Europe but also because Livy had developed symptoms of congestive heart failure. It was hoped that she could recover her health at European spas and under the care of German doctors.

In 1895–1896, Twain embarked on a lecture/reading tour aimed at paying off debts. He, his wife, and his daughter Clara traveled westward across the United States and thence to Australia, New Zealand, Southeast Asia, India, and Africa. Settling finally in England, he wrote his fifth travel book, *Following the Equator* (1897). Susy died of meningitis in Hartford just prior to the family's arrival in England, a bitter blow from which Livy never recovered and which darkened even further Twain's view of the human condition. In 1897, the family moved from London to Vienna to enable Clara to study voice and piano. They remained abroad until late 1900, when, attempting to set up life in the United States again, they settled in New York City. Twain had become a leading member of the Anti-Imperial League during the Spanish-American War of 1898, and by 1900 he began to speak out strongly against American occupation of the Philippines and other imperial adventures. By 1902, Livy's health had deteriorated radically. In ill-advised hope of warm weather, the family went to Florence for the winter of 1903–1904, where Livy died.

Now, after approximately twelve years of intermittent European exile, Twain moved back to New York City, where he had good friends such as Howells and H.H. Rogers, a Standard Oil partner and businessman. Rogers had supervised Twain's finances since 1895, guiding him into **solvency**, and now negotiated a lucrative arrangement with Harper & Row that guaranteed Twain a handsome annual **retainer** to publish exclusively with Harper and its magazines. An international celebrity, Twain became a widely sought-after and responsive semipublic New York figure, a frequently featured speaker for charitable and political causes who testified before Congressional committees, particularly about copyright legislation, and was regularly featured in newspaper stories and commercial advertisements. Though he fulfilled his writing commitment

Mark Twain received an honorary degree from Oxford University on a visit to the United Kingdom in 1907.

to Harper, much of his obsessive writing between 1904 and 1909 he devoted to his extensive autobiographical notebooks, selections from which he published. The autobiography also became the repository of a variety of fictional and non-fictional book-length works that he chose not to publish.

In 1907, Twain traveled to England, where he took great pleasure in receiving an honorary degree from Oxford University and met with the literary celebrities of the day. The next year he moved into what would be his last home, an elaborate Italian-style palazzo built for him in Redding, Connecticut. A life-long habitual cigar smoker, he indulged his habits, which included endless games of billiards, as much as was feasible in the face of a serious heart condition. The restorative powers of his favorite vacation place, Bermuda, were insufficient to compensate for his illness during his last visit there in early 1910. He returned to Redding in a wheelchair and died at home on April 21, 1910.

2

THE RIVER

A primal location for the genesis of Mark Twain as a writer, the Mississippi River, became an American possession with the Louisiana Purchase of 1803. The continent's only north–south river **conduit**, it became an essential artery of the American economy, contributing to the expansion and unification of the country, especially with the start of the steamboat age in the 1820s. By the 1840s, the river and its steamboats had become an icon, mythologized in the imagination of Americans throughout the nation.

Q. Why did the Mississippi River become so central to your life and writings?

When I was a child in Hannibal every boy had only one permanent ambition—to be a steamboat man. When the circus came, we all wanted to become clowns. When the minstrel show came, we all wanted to go on the stage. These ambitions faded away, but the ambition to be a steamboat man always remained. Every day a boat came up-river from St. Louis and another down-river from Keokuk, Iowa. The whole town waited with hushed anticipation. I can picture that moment now just as it was then: the white town drowsing in the sunshine of a summer's morning …

The Mississippi steamboat was central to the economy of the United States before the Civil War.

the majestic, magnificent Mississippi, rolling its mile-wide tide along, shining in the sun. Then someone would shout out that the boat was coming. The whole town suddenly awakened. Crowds of people and horses and cats hurried down to the wharf as the boat came into view, its flags flying. Ten minutes later it would be under way again. I would have given everything to leave as a pilot. It was the grandest position of all. It was also the most highly paid.

Q. What steps did you take to try to fulfill this ambition?

Lots of boys in town went on the river in one capacity or another. But my parents wouldn't let me. When I was eighteen, I ran away to St. Louis, swearing I'd never come home again until I was a pilot and could come in glory. I couldn't manage it, though. I got the cold shoulder at the wharves in St. Louis, where the steamboats were packed together like sardines. I went away and comforted myself with the daydream that the time would come when I should be a great and honored pilot, with plenty of money…

Q. You did become a cub pilot eventually, didn't you, which was a difficult and desirable position to get—though not before trying your hand at various other trades?

I'd learned the printer's trade, starting as an apprentice when I was thirteen. Then I worked setting type and writing some humorous stories for my brother Orion, who had bought a newspaper in Hannibal. When I ran away to go on the river and found that nobody wanted to take me on in any capacity on a steamboat, I was too embarrassed to go home. But I could find work as a printer. And since typesetters were

The pilot was the absolute master aboard a steamboat. The wheel on the *Colonel Crossman* was much larger than this one on the *Duchess*, photographed in 1887.

needed everywhere, I could see the country and pay my way. I worked in St. Louis, then New York, Philadelphia, Keokuk, and finally Cincinnati. Some newspapers printed little sketches and travel letters that I wrote. Then I bought passage on a steamboat going from Cincinnati to New Orleans, intending to sail to South America, where I had read there were great opportunities. I was fired with a longing to ascend the Amazon. If I couldn't be a steamboat pilot, at least I could have adventures and get rich.

Q. So what happened?

I found out there wasn't any ship leaving from New Orleans for South America, that there never had been any. I asked

A steamboat's arrival was a big event every day in towns along the Mississippi River.

Horace Bixby, the pilot of the steamboat I'd taken from Cincinnati, to take me on as an apprentice pilot. It took a lot of persuading, $100 down, plus another $400 from future wages. As the *Colonel Crossman* steamed away from the

levee, Bixby said, "Here, take her." My heart was pounding, my hands trembling. That's how you learned the river.

Q. Did you like Bixby?

On a steamboat the pilot was the absolute master. His word was law. And for a cub pilot the concern was survival, not affection. Bixby had an explosive temper. When it was up, he would send me and everyone working on the boat shivering. At first, every time he gave me the wheel, I either came near chipping off the edge of a plantation, or I yawed too far from shore, and so dropped back into disgrace again and got abused. I wanted to quit. "No," Bixby said. "When I say I'll learn a man the river, I mean it... I'll learn him or kill him." He learned me, even though I sometimes thought the boat would wreck while he was doing it.

Q. What did he mean by "learn the river?"

The river was always changing, always moving, cutting open new channels, silting up old ones, getting confounded with wrecks and snags and barriers and sand bars, so that every passage from New Orleans to St. Louis and back required adjusting one's knowledge. At night and when the weather changed and from season to season it was a different river. And from the start it all had to be memorized. I was in despair at first. How can you tell the different appearances and moods apart, how can you know the difference between a **wind reef** and a **bluff reef** when they look alike to ordinary eyes?

Bixby's answer: it's an instinct that comes naturally by and by. That turned out to be true, though I never lost my fear. The face of the water, in time, became a wonderful book—a book that was a dead language to an uneducated passenger, but which told its mind to me without reserve and which had a new story to tell every day for the entire four years I was on the river.

Q. So the river became a book for you to read and learn from? And you wrote books out of your river experience?

Yes, the people who worked on the river and traveled on it and lived alongside it provided me with all the different types of human nature that are to be found in fiction, biography, or history. The whole river valley, from my hometown down to St. Louis and New Orleans, gave me *The Adventures of Tom Sawyer* (1876), *The Adventures of Huckleberry Finn*, *Life on the Mississippi*, and *Pudd'nhead Wilson*—not only the towns along the shore and the situations and the voices of the people, but also the river as an image of time and change and life and death. When I find a well-drawn character in fiction or biography, I generally take a warm interest in him, for the reason that I have known him before—met him on the river.

Q. Why did you give up being a pilot?

The war closed the river in 1861. I went west to Nevada with my brother Orion, looking for new adventures and hoping to get rich. But it near broke my heart to leave the river, and in a sense I never did. *Huckleberry Finn* probably wouldn't have existed if it weren't for my steamboat days. I returned to the actual river in 1883 to write *Life on the Mississippi*, a book about the river and about myself as a young man who dreamed of becoming a steamboat pilot. For the rest of my life I dreamed about returning to it. I've said many times that it was the best time of my life.

Q. Was it really?

No—I was always afraid that I'd crack up my boat and
be disgraced. Otherwise it was wonderful. There has been
nothing comparable to it in my life since. I was young.
Fogs and dark nights had a charm for me. I didn't own any
stock in that steamboat. And that's one of the advantages
of youth. You don't own stock in anything. You have a good
time, and all the grief and trouble is with the other fellows.

Q. Why didn't you go back to the river after the war?

The time had passed for me, and for the river steamer.
I was already a writer, with the prospect of a career, and
it was becoming clear to me that I wasn't going to get
rich in Nevada working mines or investing in them, and I
couldn't go back to the river anyway because the railroads
were squeezing out the riverboats. Nevada was dry, dusty,
exhausting, but it also had wonderful characters so colorful
that no writer could invent them. Everyone wanted to strike
it rich or get rich from other people striking it rich. I kept
my stocks, which afterwards proved almost worthless, went
to the office of the *Virginia City Territorial Enterprise*, and
asked them if they'd like to hire an experienced reporter and
excellent writer. That was the start of Mark Twain.

3

SAMUEL CLEMENS BECOMES MARK TWAIN

amuel Clemens' use of a **pseudonym** has generated interest about whether Twain can best be viewed as a divided personality, the conventional Samuel Clemens and the unconventional Mark Twain, or whether the pseudonym left him no more divided than anyone else—the "singular Mark Twain." His attachment to the pseudonym was such that he used it in both public and private circumstances, alternating in private between his birth name and his self-attributed name. His family and friends knew him and addressed him as both.

Q. There's some controversy about the origin of your pseudonym, and apparently you've given different accounts of it. Please can you clarify this once and for all?

Well, since it was a made-up name I felt free to make up a story about how I made it up. Actually, I made up two stories. In Virginia City saloons it was the custom for the drinks account to be kept by making chalk marks on a board. It was usual for the bartender to allow two drinks before he required payment. So "two marks" became "Mark Twain." The other story is the one I've told more often. It was the

The young Mark Twain became a writer when his attempts to strike it rich digging for gold and silver didn't pan out.

nom de plume of a riverboat captain, one of whose articles I burlesqued in the *New Orleans Picayune*. Since he had recently died when I needed a name to put under my articles in the *Virginia City Territorial Enterprise* and my own name wouldn't do, I remembered "Mark Twain" and decided to use it. It sounded good. When I was a Mississippi riverboat pilot, every time the man taking soundings pulled up the lead and shouted out "mark twain"—which meant that we had only 12 feet (3.6 meters) of water under us, since each "mark" is 6 feet (1.8 m)—I was terrified that I'd be responsible for running the boat aground.

Q. Why couldn't you use your own name?

It was fashionable in the 1860s and '70s for humorists to use pen names, like my friend David Locke, who called himself Petroleum Vesuvius Nasby, and Charles Browne, who used the name Artemus Ward. Maybe it was because humor was considered a low form of literature. The person behind the author might not like to be associated with the category. Sometimes the name itself was funny. In my own case, I needed cover because there were some pretty tough, mean, strong-fisted, gun-carrying people in Virginia City who didn't take kindly to being satirized or exposed. If one of them came into the newspaper office breathing fire and my colleagues said, "Yes, he's here. That's Mark Twain," I could say, "No, I'm Sam Clemens."

Q. Would you have been believed?

Not at all, but afterwards the assailant could have claimed he killed the wrong man. Instead of justifiable homicide, it would have been just a mistake. I was only trying to keep him from prison.

Q. How did you evolve from a newspaperman into an author?

Newspaper standards were loose in Nevada and California in the 1860s. And the notion was that if you could find a story, you'd embellish it and provide a point of view. Usually mine was comic satire or angry outrage at injustice, especially at corrupt politicians and police chiefs. Sometimes they didn't like what I said and I had to get out of town quickly. That happened once in San Francisco when the police, who were mostly Irish, brutalized the Chinese, who were entirely helpless. Newspapermen, of course, weren't thought of as authors. I was restless and wanted to travel. And newspapers in those days regularly printed what they called "travel letters" about faraway places that Americans were interested in but had no other way of knowing much about. So, in 1866, I got hired by a California newspaper to go to Hawaii to write travel letters. A few years later I went to Europe and the Middle East.

I became an author, I suppose, when I revised the letters into my first two books—the first, that is, apart from a collection of newspaper sketches under the title about the jumping frog, which didn't sell more than a few copies. The first travel book, about the ship of pious fools going to the Holy Land, sold very well and made me an author. The trip was advertised as "The Grand Holy Land Pleasure Excursion" but I called it "The Grand Holy Land Funeral Procession." The only thing we were missing was a corpse.

4

MONEY

The coauthor of a novel called *The Gilded Age* (1873), Twain gave voice to his and his country's preoccupation with material success. From the presidency of Andrew Jackson in the 1820s to the start of the Civil War in 1861, America's economic system had evolved from rural self-sufficiency to an industrialized market economy. The application of engineering technology through inventions and improvements became a hallmark of American prosperity. Getting rich in this Protestant can-do world seemed to many a personal, social, and even religious obligation. In this regard, Twain shared the capitalist **ethos** of such entrepreneurs as Andrew Carnegie, Henry Clay Frick, John D. Rockefeller, and Thomas Edison.

Q. Has the drive for material success been important to you?

I always wanted to be rich. I went West as a young man in the hope—the expectation—that I'd strike the Mark Twain mother lode in the silver and gold mines of Nevada. I didn't intend to be a writer. I intended to strike it rich. It didn't work out. So I became a newspaperman. I hated to do it.

Mark Twain admired rich men such as Andrew Carnegie, and aspired to be one of them.

Twain's investment in the Paige Compositor didn't pay off because the machine broke down often.

But I couldn't find honest employment. It's not the spending, though, it's the joy of getting that attracts me.

Q. So you were fascinated by money?

Not by money, though the lack of money is the root of all evil. I was fascinated with the thrill and the satisfaction of getting rich, with being a successful entrepreneur. I wanted to do what my father couldn't. And in the pursuit of wealth I felt deliciously American, as if the blood of the country was pulsing in my veins. I loved the excitement of speculation. I wanted also to provide handsomely for my family, to give them everything. But the passion was there before I had even the thought of a family.

Q. Were you successful?

I made a substantial amount of money from my writing but lost much of it on bad investments, especially on inventions.

I thought that if you marketed a better mousetrap you'd become rich. I discovered that it ain't so. I tried my hand at inventions myself. One of them was a self-pasting photograph album. I made some money, but only a little. The invention I mostly wagered on, may its inventor rot in Hell, was the Paige typesetting machine. It was superior to the competition. It was the height of perfection and beauty—when it worked. And, oh Lord, that wasn't often enough! I fell in love with the machine. But it turned out to be too complicated and broke down regularly, like an overstressed human being.

I thought I could make a fortune in business, including my own publishing company, which I founded and bankrolled. Unfortunately, we are always more anxious to be distinguished for a talent which we do not possess than to be praised for the fifteen which we do possess. As I told my brother Orion, it's human nature to yearn to be what we were never intended for.

Q. Was it entirely your fault that these ventures failed?

Well, put it this way: there are many scapegoats for our blunders, but the most popular is **Providence**.

5

PROVIDENCE AND TRAINING

Twain was attracted to the theories of biological and philosophical **determinism** that arose in the nineteenth century, particularly in Europe, as a reaction against the **Romantic idealism** of the previous period and the long-standing optimism about free will in some Christian theologies. The **Calvinism** that hovered in his family background may have contributed to his determinism, a **secular** variant of Calvinistic **predestination**. He read widely and deeply in the subject, and corresponded with eminent theorists. He had a strong sense that chance had produced "turning points" in his life, and that the choices a person makes are the result of genetic and environmental circumstances rather than free will.

Q. Do you blame Providence for your failures?

You're damned right I do, but not in the ordinary sense of that word. I take full responsibility but at the same time no responsibility at all. The general view is that when a man arrives at great prosperity, God did it; when he falls into disaster, he did it himself. I don't believe in free will. I'm a determinist. It's my private gospel.

Mark Twain was given part ownership of the *Buffalo Courier* newspaper as a wedding gift. He was joined by Civil War correspondent and author George Alfred Townsend (left) and David Gray, editor of the paper, for this 1871 photo.

Q. What are its claims?

It's a philosophy, based on reason, observation, and science, that says that heredity, environment, and education—what I call "training"—determine all human thought and action. It's the dominant force: everything we are is trained into us. Training is everything. The peach was once a bitter almond; cauliflower is nothing but cabbage with a college education. In that sense, we do not have free will. Circumstances make man, not man circumstances. And human beings are not individually responsible for all their virtues and vices. People shouldn't be praised for doing good or condemned for doing evil. All these standards are delusions. I wrote about this at length in the form of a Socratic dialogue called *What Is Man?*, which I published in 1906 in an anonymous edition. But it's the main theme of *A Connecticut Yankee in King Arthur's Court.* Perhaps that's why that novel didn't sell very well. People don't like to hear these truths. Anyway—never tell the truth to people who aren't worthy of it: it will always get you in trouble.

Q. Are you claiming that training so influences our thoughts and acts that it can actually mold us into what it wants us to be?

Yes. There is nothing that training cannot do. It can turn bad morals to good, good morals to bad. It can destroy principles, it can recreate them. And it can do any one of these miracles in a year—even in six months.

Q. This is a rather bleak way of thinking. Did your philosophy bring you happiness?

Not in the least.

Mark Twain and his wife Olivia Clemens had three daughters.

Q. You've been accused of being a pessimist. Is there any truth to that?

What's an optimist? A person who travels on nothing from nowhere to happiness. Optimism is a species of daydreaming. It's always a wish and never a reality. Anyone who has eyes to see and ears to hear, who isn't a daydreaming fool, is a pessimist. But for some people it takes time to give up hoping and fantasizing. At fifty a man can be an ass without being an optimist, but not an optimist without being an ass. I stopped being an optimist long before I was fifty, except in the area of business and investments. That's where I did my daydreaming, and I paid a heavy price. With wisdom comes pessimism.

Q. Didn't you at one time think of yourself as lucky?

I thought of myself as lucky during my early years. When my younger brother, Henry, was killed in a steamboat explosion in 1858, he was on that boat and I wasn't by the merest accident of something I had arranged. I knew myself lucky. But I felt that he had died instead of me. So someone else paid a price for my luck. Life became punishing when I lost my infant son, and even more miserably so when two of my daughters and my wife died. I lost most of the money we had, even Livy's inheritance. I kept thinking I'd make it back, that my ship would come in. It seemed to be on the horizon and almost into port a number of times. Poor Livy! I was to blame, but so were the ingrates I trusted, like that scoundrel Paige, may he roast in Hell forever, and my nephew-by-marriage, Webster, whom I trusted and who betrayed me. Yes, it's all so disappointing.

Still, better a broken promise than none at all.

In the end, the promises that we think life has made to us are always broken. That's because life has never made those promises. But, especially when we're young, we think it has.

Q. You're a world-renowned author who'll be famous as long as literature written in English is still read. Aren't you proud of your accomplishment, and shouldn't that make you less of a pessimist?

I don't take credit. Sometimes I've been filled with pride and happiness. It's only momentary. And I didn't set out to be a famous writer. I never set a course and planned a career. By temperament, I was the kind of person who does things. Does them, and reflects afterwards. At each one of the turning points in my life that eventually brought me to where I am, I didn't plan the next step. Circumstances do the planning for us all. And in combination with our temperaments they determine what happens to us. One link leads to another, from Adam to the present.

Q. Any examples from your life?

When I was a boy, I crawled into bed with a playmate sick with measles. I thought I'd get it over with rather than always worrying I'd catch it. The worry was killing me.

Then I got sick to death. Everybody believed I would die. But on the fourteenth day a change came for the worse—I started to get better—and so they were disappointed. Circumstances beyond my control kept me from dying.

When I became a printer, I wandered around seeking work, as necessity required. Necessity is a circumstance. Necessity is the mother of "taking chances." I read a book about the Amazon and was fired up to go, but circumstance prevented that. Instead of going to South America I stayed in New Orleans, where I needed a job desperately. A man I'd met on the way down agreed to teach me to become a river pilot. When the war ended that, I went to Nevada because my brother was going. It was because I went to Nevada that I became a newspaper writer. I hadn't set out to be that either.

Circumstance, of course, always has a partner—temperament, a man's natural disposition. And a person's temperament is not his invention, he's born into it, and he has no authority over it, neither is he responsible for its acts. He cannot change it, nothing can change it… except temporarily. But it won't stay modified. Blue eyes are gray, in certain unusual lights, but they resume their natural color when that stress is removed.

Q. It seems as if you haven't quite worked out what you think the balance is between temperament and training?

No one ever will.

6

HUMOR, SATIRE, AND HUMAN NATURE

I n the late 1860s, Twain established himself as a Western humorist, a category that emphasized dialect, exaggeration, and a deadpan presentation of outrageous claims or actions. He soon transcended Western humor and became a national voice, adding irony and pithy wit to his other devices, and developing into a **satirist**. Always concerned about his standing among the East Coast **literati** who determined literary reputations, he resented his dismissal as a mere humorist. He cherished his friendship with the author and critic William Dean Howells, for example, because Howells used his well-placed pen to argue for Twain's literary importance, eventually describing him as "the Lincoln of our literature."

Q. Humor and satire seem to be your favorite modes for exposing falsehood. Have you been successful?

Have I influenced people to become better people, to become more honest and moral? Remember, there are political morals, commercial morals, ecclesiastical morals, and morals. The last of these will always be in short supply.

Clara Clemens (foreground) studied the piano. Her friend, Marie Nichols, stands in the background.

Human beings have a limitless capacity for rationalizing and justifying any behavior that suits their self-interest. Take, for example, commercial morality. The low level it has reached in America is deplorable. We have humble God-fearing Christian men among us who will stoop to do things for a million dollars that they ought not to be willing to do for less than two million. They set a poor example. And some of them are disagreeable. As a matter of fact, when I reflect upon the number of disagreeable people who I know have gone to a better world, I am moved to lead a different life.

Q. Don't you have any sympathy for the people you criticized?

Yes, a great deal. They too had to suffer through this existence. Why is it that we rejoice at birth and grieve at a funeral? It is because we are not the person involved.

Q. Most readers don't know about this side of you. Or at least they prefer to read the books you've written about more pleasant subjects.

Most readers think of me as that slyly funny, cheerful fellow from Hannibal, Missouri, an all-American wag from the Midwest who makes them feel good about being an American, someone "Known to Everyone—Liked by All." That's the phrase in one of those commercial advertisements that uses my picture and name without paying me anything. It's because they've only read or heard of *Tom Sawyer* or maybe *Huckleberry Finn,* and even *Huck* is a pretty dark book. The truth is that they shouldn't feel good about being human beings at all. We're a pretty nasty bunch with occasional exceptions. Keep in mind that if you pick up a starving dog and make him prosperous, he won't bite you. This is the principal difference between a dog and a man.

Q. So you don't think much of human nature?

I've published some harsh essays and stories about human nature, like "Corn-pone Opinions" and "The Man That Corrupted Hadleyburg." They don't sell well, especially compared to my travel books, in which my satire and my determinism are disguised by travel adventures and lots of interesting descriptions. *The Innocents Abroad*, my first book, was a great success. Ever since, the sales of my books have gone gradually and then sharply down. *A Connecticut Yankee in King Arthur's Court* and *Pudd'nhead Wilson* sold poorly. If there was such a thing as a bestseller list, they wouldn't be on it.

Q. How would you describe yourself as a writer? Are you a humorist?

No, I'm not a humorist—though I often use humor—but a satirist, a moralist, and a teacher. A key characteristic of the human species is its inability to learn, so the attempt to teach has its strict limits. Keep in mind that clothes make the man. Naked people have little or no influence in society. That's a humorous comment, isn't it? But it's also satirical and moralistic. It tries to influence people not to be naked, by which I mean you've got to wear clothes of some kind or other because naked anything, especially the naked truth, isn't acceptable. But it's nakedness—frankness, honesty, sincerity—that should be respected. Our society, though, isn't comfortable with that. People don't want to see or hear or read nakedness. So humor helps a writer disguise and make more palatable what he wants to say. Of course, if it's nothing but humor, it stops there.

Q. Didn't you get some advantage from being labeled a humorist?

For a good part of my career, especially until the 1890s, readers labeled me as a humorist, by which they meant I was funny and mostly harmless. My wife resented that I was being classified as a lightweight—that's what being a humorist meant. Still, it was humor that often brought in the audiences, and when they stayed they got plenty more than humor. They got some truths about the human condition. I always kept in mind as a writer and human being that to be good is noble, but to show others how to be good is nobler, and no trouble.

Mark Twain in the library of his Connecticut home. Olivia Clemens wanted her husband to be thought of as more than a humorist.

7

RELIGION, GOD, AND THE BIBLE

Twain falls into a nineteenth century category of "honest doubters." The Christianity that they had been raised in seemed unsatisfactory, yet they also felt their loss of belief deeply. Such unorthodoxy, however, could affect a writer's livelihood. Writers like Twain, Thomas Carlyle, Walt Whitman, and Ralph Waldo Emerson evolved strategies to incorporate their **heterodox** beliefs into their writings. Sometimes, Twain used God as a literary device, a convenient frame for comments about human nature. At other times, he made clear that he had an argument with a God responsible for such a human and cosmic mess. For satirical purposes, he treated God as incompetent or as a fiction created by religions to manipulate believers.

Q. What's your view of religion?

All religion is folly. And the easy confidence with which I know another man's religion is folly teaches me to suspect that my own is also. Still, I wouldn't interfere with anyone's religion, either to strengthen or to weaken it. Folly as it is, it may be a great comfort to him in this life—hence it's a valuable possession to him.

The Church of the Holy Sepulchre, shown in this photo from around 1900, has been a primary destination for pilgrims to Jerusalem for centuries.

Q. Do you literally believe in God and Satan?

All my life I've doubted the existence of God and Satan
as anything but human inventions. God is not interesting,
even as a literary character or as a figment of the everyday
imagination. But Satan is. I've written about him at length
in a series of stories that I began in Vienna in 1897. One of
them is about "young Satan." The main idea is that Satan
appears in an Austrian village in 1490 and plays havoc
with the inhabitants, revealing the limitations of human
nature and clerical folly. I had a hard time coming up with a
title—the best I could think of was "No. 44, The Mysterious
Stranger." I also tried a version set in contemporary America,
in a village very like my boyhood home of Hannibal,
Missouri. And I wrote about Satan in *Letters from the Earth*
(published posthumously as a collection in 1962).

Q. Why are you so fascinated by Satan?

Satan is a great human creation, full of interest and literary
possibility. I believed in him literally as a boy and cowered
under the covers when I thought he might be coming.
He's the representative of a powerful force of attraction
and repulsion in our psyches. In that sense, he's real.
And he's very useful to show how stupid and irrational
and superstitious and cruel human beings are.

Q. When you talk about God, which God do you mean?

Well, the God I grew up with was a Protestant God.
That God is the one given to us by the Bible and the
sacred books of other religions and then developed by the
churches. In all my travels, the local gods always had a lot

in common with our American Protestant deity. Except in Hawaii and India, where there are so many of them... And worship is more sensibly arranged. The Hawaiians give their gods a helping hand. For example, there was a temple devoted to prayers for rain—and with rare sagacity it was placed at a point so well up in the mountainside that if you prayed there twenty-four times a day for rain you'd be likely to get it every time. You'd seldom get to your "Amen" before you'd have to hoist your umbrella.

Q. What's your view of the monotheistic **gods, such as Jehovah and Allah?**

When I visited Palestine and traveled in the Muslim world, I couldn't see much difference between Jehovah and Allah. They're both very demanding and always favor those who bribe them the most. It's a funny thing, isn't it, how much these gods like gifts? When I was a boy, I hid under the bedclothes when lightning flashed because I'd been told that God would punish me if I did bad things—if I didn't read the Bible and didn't go to church and if I did the things that little boys do, like be greedy and eat too much candy and pull girls' pigtails.

Q. And did you do these bad things?

There wasn't a boy in Hannibal who tried as much to be good as I did but who couldn't help doing bad things! That's the problem with so much of our training: it tries to get us to do unnatural things. Almost all the people I knew in Hannibal were Protestants, with a lot of doom and gloom and you-better-mind-your-ways and hell-fire preaching.

Yes, when I talk about God I mean God in general, since he seems to show up in the same way in most human cultures. But I was drenched in Protestant Christianity, as were most Americans of my generation, and so it's that God whose words and deeds and influence are most in my mind when I mention the deity.

Q. How were your views about the literal truths expressed in the Bible—such as the Genesis account of Creation—affected by the new evidence emerging from geology, astronomy, and biology—by the ideas of Darwin, for example?

When I went to Palestine as a young man in 1868, I had a long time before I concluded that the Bible is one of the least trustworthy accounts of how human beings came into existence. In Palestine, I was taken to a geologically striated cut in a mountain I was told was Noah's Mount Ararat. There were oyster shells in regular layers 500 feet (152 m) above the sea. After dismissing the possibility that Noah and his family had eaten all those oysters and thrown the shells overboard, I was painfully, even humiliatingly, reduced to one slender theory: that the oysters climbed up there of their own accord. But what object could they have had in view? What did they want up there? What could any oyster want to climb a hill for? To climb a hill must necessarily be a fatiguing and annoying exercise for an oyster. The most natural conclusion would be that the oysters climbed up there to look at the scenery. Yet when one comes to reflect upon the nature of an oyster, it seems plain that he does not care for scenery.

A trip to Palestine in 1868 provided material for Mark Twain's first travel book *The Innocents Abroad*.

Q. Don't you believe that God created man?

Put it this way, if you will: I believe that our Heavenly Father invented man because he was disappointed in the monkey. He was equally disappointed in man when he realized that he was no considerable improvement upon the monkey.

8

THE WRITER

Twain's productivity in various literary forms was characteristically Victorian. In his lifetime, he was widely thought of as a writer who transcended genres. His living as a writer and his fame as a celebrity resulted from the success of his travel books, his caustically satirical essays, his journalism, his appearances as a lecturer and after-dinner speaker, and his works of fiction, which sold less well than his travel books. Eventually, the works and the personality became inseparable in the public mind. He became known for being Mark Twain, a national and international celebrity.

Q. Let's get back to the kind of writer you are, and to your books. First, how did you manage to write so much, and what were your writing habits?

Those of us who make a living at writing work hard at it or we don't make a living, and some of those who work hard at it don't make a living anyway. Many who think they have the calling don't—they'd be better off selling lemonade in winter. I thought I could do it, and it turned out that I could. After all, it was better than the alternatives. When I first tried to make a living as a writer, I'd been breaking my back with a pickaxe trying to get silver and gold out of the ground.

Mark Twain, pictured here in his study in 1903, worked hard to make his writing appear simple.

I hadn't wanted to be a writer. I never had but two powerful ambitions in my life. One was to be a riverboat pilot, and the other a preacher of the gospel. I accomplished the one and failed in the other, because I couldn't supply myself with the necessary stock in trade. When prestigious literary editors praised my sketches, I began to believe that I had a talent for humorous writing. I wrote so much partly because that's how I made my living. Otherwise, I'd have preferred to have given in to my innate laziness. Let's save tomorrows for work.

Q. Was writing always work?

It was work only when I had to do it. It caused me irritation and resentment beyond description whenever I had a task imposed on me. I felt like I was bound into slavery and about to explode in rebellion. That's how I was from childhood. If I was told to do something, that very act made me want not to do it. But I still had to do it—more and more of it as I needed money for a family.

Writing gave me a lot of freedom. Sometimes it was play. But work and play are words used to describe the same thing under differing conditions.

Q. But you didn't have to keep the dozens of notebooks you kept over your lifetime and you didn't have to write all the stories you knew you wouldn't publish. And what about the million or more words of autobiography that you wrote over the years?

Writing when it becomes a habit is hard to break, like all habits. You can straighten a worm but the crook is in him and only waiting. It's also hard to separate a habit from a compulsion, something you do because it defines who you are to yourself. And when the doing gives you pleasure also, then compulsion, necessity, and pleasure become inseparable. Once I was set in my ways, I couldn't stop.

Q. Do you feel satisfied with your success as a writer?

It isn't likely that any complete life has ever been lived which wasn't a failure in the secret judgment of the person that lived it.

Q. You have the reputation of being a natural writer— of writing coming easy to you and of not needing to revise. Is that so? In the minds of some high-class critics, you're thought of almost as a primitive writer.

All successful writing is artifice. It takes a lot of practice and hard work to create the impression that what you do is haphazard and unplanned. I specialize in the art of seeming artless. So those who think I'm a primitive writer are those with whom I've most succeeded as an artist. Which doesn't mean that I over-think things. I trust to the truthfulness of my feelings and the strength of my gift. But I always revise. In fact, the time to begin writing an article is when you've finished it to your satisfaction.

Q. Do you have any more advice for young writers?

Oh, Lordy, that question again? I always answered the questions I got from aspiring writers by saying, don't—unless you can't help yourself. It's not likely to make you happy or rich. Write what you know about, and write it in the most economical and precise way you can. Keep in mind some of the nineteen cardinal rules I state in my essay on "Fenimore Cooper's Literary Offenses."

Q. Which are?

Say exactly what you're proposing to say, don't merely come near it; use the right word, not its second cousin; eschew surplusage; don't omit necessary details; avoid slovenliness of form; use good grammar; employ a simple and straightforward style. For writers of tales there are special rules, like a tale should accomplish something and arrive somewhere, and when the characters have conversations it should sound like human talk.

But I'm not about to repeat all the rules here. Read the essay. It's been widely reprinted.

Q. It's said that you were one of the first well-known writers to use a new invention called the typewriter. Is that true?

Yes. In 1874, I bought one of the first machines made by the Remington Company. It typed only capital letters. My first effort stated that I AM TRYING T TO GET THE HANG OF THIS NEW F FANGLED WRITING MACHINE. BUT AM NOT MAKING A SHINING SUCCESS OF IT.

Q. Did you go on to make a success out of it?

Yes. I love inventions. Have you got one I can invest in?

Remington started production on its first typewriter in 1873, and Mark Twain bought one the next year.

9

THE CULTURAL CRITIC

An autodidact who read widely in social, psychological, and philosophical literature, Twain found that his sophistication as cultural critic was initially obscured by his reputation as a humorist. By the late 1880s, he had created a body of work whose intellectual sharpness and thematic emphases established him as one of the major nineteenth century cultural commentators. He fitted into a characteristically Victorian role, similar to that of Charles Dickens and John Ruskin, writers who like Twain took as their targets governmental corruption, rampant materialism, **philistinism**, social stultification, Christian hypocrisy, and the flawed manners and mores of Anglo-American society.

Q. You seem to have made a career of rebuking your countrymen about their moral, political, and international behavior.

They provide plenty of cause. My mission in life is to correct other people's mistakes. It costs me nothing and makes me popular among those who agree with me.

Q. How do you get away with it?

Well, first, I always acknowledge my faults frankly. It throws those in authority off their guard and gives me the opportunity to commit more. Humor helps. People don't like to be laughed at, so they tend to stop at the humor and not go on to the criticism. That way they're easy on me and easy on themselves.

Q. Doesn't that undercut your effectiveness? Aren't you trying to make the world a better place?

No, because a long time ago I gave up on that possibility for the majority of the human race. There's no such thing as progress in morals. Maybe the world's a slightly better place because people can enjoy my performances. But human nature doesn't change. Everybody's private motto is: It's better to be popular than right. I try to be both.

Q. That can't be easy.

No, few things are harder to put up with than the annoyance of a good example. And honesty isn't easy, either. It was the best policy. And it's the best of all the lost arts. Fiction is more truthful than fact—my fiction, I mean. A good story is the highest truth. And, as I said before, never tell the truth to people who aren't worthy of it—it's bad for them and will get you in trouble.

Q. In *The Innocents Abroad*, your account of a five-month visit to Europe and the Holy Land with a group of religious pilgrims, you don't seem to pull many

The piety of religious pilgrims provided an easy target for Mark Twain's pen in *The Innocents Abroad*.

punches about the manners and hypocrisy of your pious fellow travelers.

Those Presbyterians were an easy and relatively safe target. I didn't take it so far as to directly deny Christian claims and practices that were clearly preposterous, such as the Virgin Birth. But I slyly raised questions.

Hypocrites are easy targets. Most of my fellow passengers were vandals, picking up ancient shards and artifacts from the sites we visited as if they were there for the taking, behaving like smug barbarians perplexed by the oddness and undesirability of foreign customs. The trick of the book

Mark Twain could hold his own in a game of billiards.

was for me as the narrator to be both one of them in my occasional tongue-in-cheek innocence and at the same time to expose the cultural **egocentricity**, irrational faith, and human stupidity that was on such plentiful display... The trouble ain't that there's too many fools, but that the lightning ain't distributed right.

Q. Isn't there an inconsistency in your fascination with technological improvements and your depiction, at the end of *A Connecticut Yankee in King Arthur's Court*, of an apocalyptic destruction of society after the main character introduces modern weaponry into a medieval society? Isn't it the case that scientific people are sometimes as foolish and destructive as religious people?

Man has great inventive and creative capacities. His nature may not allow him to use them constructively. But blind faith, irrationalism, and the medieval mentality, which are alive and flourishing in the modern era, are the main destructive forces. In the hands of fanatics and the dishonest, these forces manipulate human nature. They beat the drums of hatred and war. They appeal to greed and cultural arrogance. It's only etiquette that requires us to admire the human race.

Q. And what of America?

Well, we've turned into a nation like any other, a little better than some, a little worse than others.

10

TRAVEL

An insatiable traveler for business, pleasure, and escape, Twain was a noteworthy contributor to a widely practiced nineteenth century Anglo-American genre. It brought European and British travel writers, such as Alexis de Tocqueville, Charles Dickens, Anthony Trollope, and William Makepeace Thackeray, to America before the Civil War and sent Americans abroad, particularly Herman Melville in 1857 and Twain in the late 1860s. The emphasis in the genre was mainly on information and cultural criticism, except for the many American accounts of travels to Palestine, with their emphasis on religious experience. Twain's distinctive contribution to the genre was the humorous and satirical inflection of *The Innocents Abroad* and *Roughing It*.

Q. Why did you like traveling so much?

I was always restless. There was also a professional reason, since I made some of my living as a travel writer. Of course, my travel books aren't only about where I went and what I saw. They're about the "I" of that sentence—about me. The reader gets to know and experience me through what I have to say about the places and people I'm visiting and

A restless Mark Twain loved to travel, and it provided him with material for his writing.

what I have to say about myself. All the travel books are autobiographical, though the most autobiographical is *Life on the Mississippi*. The first eighteen chapters are about my experiences as a river pilot. The best job I ever had. So, though it's a travel book, it's also the story of my education on the river. And it's a book about America in terms of the river and that whole Mississippi Valley region—North and South—both before and after the Civil War.

Q. What made you so restless?

To some extent natural curiosity, the thrill of anticipating distant places. For a small-town boy, the glamour of the big city and of exotic faraway places that I read about had an irresistible allure. Like *Tom Sawyer*, I was always daydreaming and exercising my imagination. That got extended into an interest in seeing how people in other cultures live and how they differ from us. When two Jewish boys came to our little school in Hannibal, I was awestruck—they were descendants of the Old Testament patriarchs whose larger-than-life pictures were in my Sunday School story book. I was puzzled, though: why didn't these ordinary-looking boys look like my pictures of Abraham and Moses? I wondered what the descendants of the patriarchs who lived in Palestine would look like.

Q. What did they look like, when you went to Palestine?

I saw that the biblical patriarchs had shrunk. So, too, had the country. I suppose it was because I could not, as a boy, conceive of a small country having so large a history. I was already in the business of writing about the gap between our delusions and the reality. Yes, my subject was the manners and customs of the places I visited, but also those of the traveler, whether I was alone or with others. I always wanted to learn and to keep learning. The world was my university. And it wasn't always getting to new places that gave me pleasure: it was also leaving old places behind. Well, even if I could never leave them entirely behind, I could have the illusion of doing so while traveling. My favorite kind of journey was a long sea voyage, the best escape from civilization, which is a limitless multiplication of unnecessary necessaries.

Mark Twain loved Hawaii, and stayed in the Volcano House during his visit.

Q. Of all the places you've traveled to, which is the place to which you'd most like to return?

I still daydream about returning to Hawaii, where I spent four blissful months in 1868 and which I wrote about in *Roughing It*—the book wasn't long enough with only the account of my days in Nevada and California, so I took my newspaper letters from Hawaii, rewrote them, and added them on to make the last section of the book. What I've always longed for was the privilege of living way up on one of those mountains, overlooking the sea. I almost did return. When we were sailing to Australia in 1895, on my round-the-world tour, our stopover in Honolulu was canceled because of quarantine. We could see the city lights, but we couldn't disembark.

Q. You've lived in many places. Why did you absent yourself from America for long periods of time, and which of the places you lived in abroad were you most at home in?

I love my country so much that I couldn't bear the pain of always living there. That is, the best lover is the best critic, and neither America nor I were always happy with one another. Anyway, you can often see your homeland more clearly from a distance.

Q. Why did you choose to live in Europe for long periods?

I stayed in Germany, Switzerland, and Italy to write about my visits, and also my wife Livy loved German music and literature. We all took German lessons. I could read the language, though I never learned to speak it well. Once when I was talking to a friend about some private matters in English because there were some Germans nearby, my friend said to me, "Speak in German, Mark. Some of these people may understand English." And we had long visits to England during the 1870s and 1880s because they loved me there and

I loved being there. To go back to your previous question, I'd say that England was the country I was most at home in other than America.

Q. You also spent some time in Austria from 1897 to 1899, didn't you?

We lived in Austria, mostly in Vienna, for almost two years, for my daughter Clara to study voice and piano with the best teachers in the world. And it suited my pocketbook, which was pressured. My finances had taken a plunge. We tried to sell the Hartford house. I thought I'd save money by living in Europe. And after my daughter Susy died in Hartford, where she'd remained while the rest of the family came with me on my round-the-world-trip, we stayed on in England—for me to write *Following the Equator* (1897), but also because there was no home to go home to. I can't think of the time when we lost her without feeling pain…

Q. Italy, also, must hold unhappy memories for you?

In 1903, we went to live in Italy again because the doctors said that a warm climate would be beneficial for my wife, Livy. She had congestive heart disease. I curse the damn doctors and their advice! Florence wasn't warm in the winter. We were miserable. And she died there. So over the years, I also came to associate travel with bankruptcy and death.

11

DOLLARS, ROYALTY, AND FAME

An **iconoclast** and wide-ranging satirist, Twain found his sense of justice offended by the gap between the founding principles of the United States and the widespread injustice in society. He considered it his mission to expose national hypocrisy, especially greed and exploitation in high places. As a newspaper columnist and travel writer, he had ample opportunity to comment on such matters.

Q. In your novel *Pudd'nhead Wilson* you wrote, "It was wonderful to find America, but it would have been more wonderful to miss it." What was it about America that disappointed you so much and led to such a bleak view?

My major disappointment is with the damned human race—America is a subcategory. But it's the one that's my own and the one I know best, so I feel I'm in a privileged position to comment on it.

Let's start with our governing class. What are politicians? Persons chosen by the people to distribute the graft. It's the criminal class of our country. Graft is what we Americans call the money or gifts that a public employee gets when he does something illegal on someone's behalf, somewhat like a

Mark Twain was on his best behavior when he met Queen Victoria of England (pictured) and other members of royal families.

bribe… And what's a senator? A person who makes laws in Washington when not doing time. I had a first-hand view of political corruption when I was a reporter in Virginia City, then in San Francisco, and then in the nation's capital. Almost everything was influence and deals and money. My novel *The Gilded Age* has as its main theme the personal and political corruption that dominates public life. It was bad before the Civil War. But when I came to Washington after the war, public office had become private graft.

Q. Isn't it human nature to be acquisitive?

Yes, and corruptible and corrupt. The general view is that it's better to take what doesn't belong to you than to let it lie around neglected. We can see the sense in that. Of course, it isn't only the American who adores the Almighty Dollar. It was a dull person who invented the idea that the American's devotion to the dollar is more strenuous than the Englishman's or the Frenchman's or the Chinaman's or anyone else's.

Q. What about those at the top of the scale of power and influence—royalty, say? You've met kings and emperors—how have they impressed you?

I've met more than a dozen assorted European and Asian royalty. Those who impressed me most were Hawaiian, because they had oddly interesting customs. Naturally, they thought our customs odd, too. But show me a king or an emperor and you'll show me a thief or someone who comes from a long line of thieves. Of course, I didn't say that to Kaiser Wilhelm or Queen Victoria or the Prince of Wales.

I can be counted on for civilized manners, even in the presence of royalty. And I always thought, isn't this amazing? What's little Sammy Clemens from Hannibal, Missouri, doing here?

Q. So you're an anti-monarchist?

Monarchy is the institutional proof that there's an innate tendency within human beings to worship power and authority.

Q. Do Americans also worship royalty?

To worship rank and privilege is the dear and valued privilege of the whole human race, and it's freely and joyfully exercised in democracies as well as in monarchies. There's something pathetic and funny about this human race's fondness for contact with power and distinction, and for the reflected glory it gets out of it. We're so obsessed with European royalty that we'd import it here if we had half the chance.

Q. As a distinguished person yourself, people must get reflected glory from you. How do you feel about that?

I enjoy being famous. In Vienna, the police shut me off with fifty other people from a street that the Emperor was about to pass through. The captain of the guard turned and saw the situation and said indignantly to them all: "Can't you see that it's the Herr Mark Twain? Let him through!" As I said at the time, it will be four hundred years before I forget the wind of self-complacency that rose in me.

12

PRESIDENTS AND POLITICIANS

With his marriage into the Langdon family and then his move to Hartford in 1872, Twain became a member of the liberal and intellectual northeastern branch of the Republican Party, which had been founded in 1854 in support of the anti-slavery movement. As an editor, columnist, letter writer, and participant in local and national attempts at social and governmental reform, from 1877 though 1890 and again from the late 1890s to 1910, he played a prominent part in contributing to public opinion on issues and people of importance.

Q. You've known American presidents. What's your view of them?

The two presidents I admired most are Grover Cleveland, a Democrat, and General Grant, a Republican. I belonged to the Republican Party for most of my life, but when it nominated someone for president—James G. Blaine—whom I thought blatantly corrupt, I bolted and became a "mugwump," a renegade Republican who supported the Democratic nominee. I voted for Cleveland twice.
After the election my wife made my daughters take off their Cleveland buttons because she didn't want anyone to think

we were Democrats. In 1868 and 1872 I supported Grant wholeheartedly, and I always admired and loved the man. Yes, there was corruption in his administration, but he himself was pure. Grant was American manhood at its best. He was our greatest general, the equal of George Washington.

Q. Did you write any part or all of General Grant's autobiography, as many people seem to believe?

No, that's a widely circulated falsehood. I didn't write a word of it. I was outraged when Grant, who desperately needed money, signed a contract with a conniving publisher that paid him far less than his memoir was worth. I knew what a good writer he was from the articles he'd published about the war in *Century Magazine*. He made a powerful style out of honest writing, out of restraint and the exact word. He knew the difference between the right word and the wrong word, the difference between lightning and the lightning bug.

I influenced him to sign with my publishing firm, Webster and Company. I gave most of the profit, which turned out to be a great deal of money, to his wife and children. The general had cancer of the throat. He won his race against the clock and finished the book just before he died. It turned out not only to be the best memoir ever written by a president or a general but a literary masterpiece.

Q. Is it possible that some of your admiration for Grant stems from the fact that having become a post-Civil War Republican you needed to distance yourself from having fought on the Confederate side?

It's an exaggeration, like premature reports of my death, to say that I fought on the Confederate side. I didn't want to have anything to do with the war. When the river was closed by Union gunboats, I just barely made it back to St. Louis and went into hiding. If the Union folks had caught me, I would have been drafted into river service for them. My home state, Missouri, was on the side of the Confederacy, so I was hiding from those people, too. If they'd found me, I feared they would have shamed me into joining them.

Q. But you did wear the Confederate uniform, didn't you?

After a while, I went up-river to Hannibal, where I joined some of my schoolboy friends. We made up part of the Marion County militia, sort of guarding things, though we didn't have uniforms. It turned out to be uncomfortable and dangerous and scary, as I wrote in "The Private History of a Campaign that Failed." We didn't know what we were doing. Then we found ourselves in the way of Colonel—later General—Grant's forces, and we knew that wasn't good for us. But we really didn't know who or what we were running from.

Q. Did you kill anyone?

We killed a Union soldier and thought that was wonderful until we went up and saw the man dying, mumbling about his wife and child. And it seemed an epitome of war: that all war must be just that—the killing of strangers against whom you feel no personal animosity. That spoiled my campaign. It seemed to me I was not rightly equipped for the awful business.

As soon as the opportunity arose, I got away. I went to Nevada with my brother Orion. So it's not really accurate to say I fought for the Confederacy. That scuppers that theory about why I admired General Grant. I was a son of Missouri, and we were a slave state. Naturally I identified with Missouri at first, but I changed gradually, and over time I didn't admire slavery and I got to believe in Lincoln and Grant and the Union and the principles of the Republican Party, except when it betrayed its principles.

Q. When did it betray its principles?

It did so in 1876, when it nominated Blaine, who was blatantly corrupt, and did so more and more as it aligned itself entirely with big business. It became the party of the wealthy and it came to believe that what was good for the party was good for America.

Q. But weren't you friends with wealthy Republicans, such as Andrew Carnegie and the oil millionaire H.H. Rogers?

I have nothing against millionaires—I wanted to be one myself. Carnegie bought fame and paid cash for it. That's very American, and sometimes admirable. When I first met him, I saw that he was not any better acquainted with himself than if he had met himself for the first time the day before yesterday. There was something refreshing about that lack of guile.

He delighted in reminding people that this is a Christian country. Why, Carnegie, so is Hell. Before I met him, I sent him a note, responding to an advertisement that he would give a hymnbook to all who requested one. "My dear Mr. Carnegie—I see by the papers that you are very prosperous. I want to get a hymnbook. It costs six shillings. I will bless you, God will bless you, and it will do a great deal of good. P.S. Don't send me the hymnbook; send me the six shillings."

Q. What about your friendship with Rogers?

One of the most dear, loyal, and generous friends of my life, and he was the most upright businessman I ever met. When I had financial problems, he put his business skill to work on my behalf, as an act of friendship, and got my financial ship righted. He negotiated with my creditors, whom we paid in full. He reminded me that my good name was my fortune. He arranged everything about my backlist with Harper, which gave me a secure annual income. That was for friendship, not money or flattery. And he was a damned good poker player, which he always beat me at. That's why I didn't like the game much. When I got him to the billiards table, which was often, I showed him who was boss. He was often maligned as one of the Standard Oil **robber barons**. To me he was just a baron, first class.

Q. Don't you admire Theodore Roosevelt?

No. He was the most infantile and egomaniacal president in my lifetime. He was the Tom Sawyer of the political world, always hunting for a chance to show off. In his frenzied imagination the Great Republic was a vast Barnum Circus with him for a clown and the whole world for an audience. He would go to Halifax for half a chance to show off, and he would go to Hell for a whole one.

Q. In your life, wasn't he the most popular president since Lincoln?

Lincoln wasn't popular even in the North until he was assassinated. The whole country was frantically fond of Roosevelt, even idolized him. He was so blindly and

Teddy Roosevelt was admired by most Americans, but not by Mark Twain.

unreasonably worshiped that I feared that his infantile personality and the public's infatuation with him were leading us down a dangerous path. In the end, we would have King Teddy. Years ago I amused myself forecasting what the country would be like when the republic was replaced by a monarchy—but I wasn't expecting it to happen in my lifetime.

Q. Aren't you being unwarrantedly alarmist?

No. It's human nature to want something definite to look up to, worship, and obey—God and King, for example. Great republics have always fallen. The rule of history always stays the rule of history. And great power and wealth breed commercial and political corruption, which encourages popular leaders to dream of becoming all-powerful rulers.

Q. But America is a democracy.

Wrong again! For fifty years our country had been a constitutional monarchy, with the Republican Party sitting on the throne. Cleveland's two terms were brief interludes— accidents, in fact. And then Roosevelt created the imperial presidency, the chief executive as king with a supine or an adulatory Congress. He had hugely enlarged the presidential entourage. He put the White House staff in uniforms and surrounded himself with a praetorian guard, like an emperor. The Republic in name remained but the republic in fact was gone.

Mr. Roosevelt and his ilk always want a war. He was in a skirmish once at San Juan Hill, and he got so much moonshine glory out of it that he was never been able to stop talking about it since. He liked to kill animals. He killed a cow. I'm sure he honestly thought it was a bear, but the circumstantial evidence that it was a cow is overwhelming. There's no heroism in killing an exhausted cow.

13

IMPERIALISM

A strong Unionist after the Civil War, Twain supported the expansion of American influence into the Caribbean and the Pacific. The war made the United States the world's foremost military-industrial power. Under President William McKinley in the 1890s, naval armaments became a budget priority. In 1898, the long-standing American interest in annexing Cuba, a Spanish possession, expressed itself in a trumped-up incident that allowed America to declare war on Spain and invade both Cuba and the Philippines, another Spanish possession. By the turn of the century the United States had become an imperial force. Twain became, with William Dean Howells and William James, one of the founders of the Anti-Imperial League.

Q. Do you view Roosevelt's military budgets as a continuation of the policies of President McKinley?

Yes, McKinley led the way. Roosevelt followed and widened it. I think all presidents hereafter will find it useful to lead America into wars to serve their own interests and ideologies. Roosevelt never saw a battleship that he didn't like and want. And he used his naval toys to provoke Japan and other countries.

Admiral George Dewey led the American naval forces against the Spanish in the Battle of Manila Bay in the Philippines in 1898.

An incident involving the USS *Maine*, entering Havana Harbor, sparked the Spanish-American War.

Q. Didn't you oppose the invasion of Cuba and the Philippines in 1898?

Not at first. I thought it a good idea to support the Cuban independence movement and expel Spain. After all, the Cubans were entitled to rule themselves and Spain had perpetuated its tyranny for centuries. But it soon turned out that we'd liberated Cuba for the purpose of turning it over to American sugar barons and the United Fruit Company. We'd gone into the colony business. It was deplorable, I opposed it, but at least it was a bloodless colonization under the guise of a puppet government.

Q. And how did you feel about the occupation of the Philippines?

I applauded Admiral Dewey's destruction of the Spanish fleet at Manila Bay. The oppressor's heel was being lifted from the neck of the oppressed. But soon it was clear that, as Howells said, "the war for humanity" had been turned "into a war for coaling stations." If we'd played the game the way we said we would, Dewey would have sailed away and left the Philippines to govern itself. But we brutally crushed the Philippine independence movement. We have got the archipelago and we shall never give it up. As for a flag, we can have a special one made up. We can use our regular flag with the white stripes painted black and the stars replaced by the skull and crossbones.

Q. Did the Americans join the British as the major international imperialists?

A few years after our occupation of the Philippines, Britain crushed the Boer movement in South Africa. When Winston Churchill, the Boer War hero, came to New York, I told the audience at a grand welcoming dinner that apparently America admired Britain so much that we were now becoming like her. Britain sinned in getting into a war in South Africa that she could have avoided without loss of credit or dignity—just as we have sinned in crowding ourselves into a war in the Philippines on the same terms.

Q. But surely American intervention in these countries, and in China, was more justified than that of the colonialist European regimes such as Germany, France,

Belgium, and even Britain, for which I know you have a soft spot?

Britain and America have always been kin—kin in blood, kin in religion, kin in representative government, kin in ideals, kin in just and lofty purposes. And now we are kin in sin, the harmony is complete, the blend is perfect. The kinship was embodied in the marriage of Mr. Churchill's American mother and English father. The great traditions of human liberty that both countries have championed at home have been traduced abroad. Is it perhaps possible that there are two kinds of civilization—one for home consumption and one for the heathen market?

Q. But doesn't Christianity bring blessings to the heathens?

They've already been blessed enough. Even if our civilization was worth exporting, what we're doing is pirating, not civilizing. On New Year's Day I toasted the new century: "I bring you the stately matron Christianity, returning bedraggled, besmirched, and dishonored from pirate-raids in Kiaochow, Manchuria, South Africa, and the Philippines, with her soul full of meanness, her pocket full of boodle, and her mouth full of pious hypocrisies. Give her soap and a towel, but hide the looking-glass."

Q. Why, in your view, has the United States taken on the imperial mantle?

Our Republican government and its business allies find these new markets irresistible. And misguided missionaries, especially in China, find that there are millions of heathens crying out for Christian salvation. Extending the Blessings of Civilization to our Brother who Sits in Darkness has been a good trade and has paid well, on the whole. And there's money in it yet, if carefully worked. And the crucial question is, shall we go on conferring our Civilization upon the people that sit in darkness, or shall we give those poor things a rest?

Q. Would you also have had American forces leave China?

Yes. The Chinese were plenty good enough as they were. And every convert runs the risk of catching our civilization. We ought to be careful. Anyway, we have plenty of need for the missionaries here. Patriotism imposes this duty on them. Our country is worse off than China.

Q. What do you mean?

In China they didn't lynch people for not being yellow. In Georgia, Alabama, Mississippi, and Louisiana we lynched people for being black. There was an epidemic of bloody insanities raging. Even the people who in their hearts were revolted stood by in the crowd, afraid to buck public opinion. When I was a boy I saw a brave gentleman deride and insult a mob and drive it away. I put that into *The Adventures of Huckleberry Finn*. A single individual who doesn't suffer from moral cowardice can control a crowd. But it's our nature to conform—it's a force which not many can successfully resist. That's human nature's commonest weakness… the inborn instinct to imitate. We should have imported American missionaries from China, and sent them into the lynching fields.

14

SLAVERY AND RACE

Political and philosophical disagreement about slavery existed from the adoption of the Constitution in 1789 to the outbreak of the Civil War. An uneasy balance between slavery and anti-slavery interests was maintained, but Southern interests agitated for the unfettered expansion of slavery. In 1861, the newly formed Republican Party came to national power on an explicitly anti-slavery platform. Twain rejected nineteenth century theories of race that elevated whites, partly because of his conviction that there was no rational basis for such claims, and also as part of his resolution of the tension between the racial prejudices of his Missouri origin and his admiration for Southern black culture.

Q. What was the general attitude toward slavery in your childhood?

When I was a boy in Missouri, no one I knew ever gave a thought to whether slavery was right or wrong. It existed as a natural part of our everyday life. Slaves worked as house servants or for farmers, and they were bought and sold. We were a poor family, though we never thought of ourselves as poor, but we occasionally had a slave. Slave traders came

Slavery was part of the culture of Missouri when Samuel Clemens was growing up.

through and there was a slave market. The slave trader was not respected. Most of the slaves were treated well, and when there was an exception the man who treated a slave badly was looked down on. My mother, the most tender-hearted of women, would almost shed tears at the unhappiness of a slave who'd been separated from his family. She told me that I should understand his unhappiness and never be harsh to that boy. But it never dawned on my mother that there was anything wrong with slavery itself or, if there were some problems, that she could do anything about them. That was the natural feeling of most everybody in Hannibal.

Q. When did you become conscious about slavery as an institution and start to think it was a bad thing?

It was a gradual process. I was always tenderhearted, couldn't stand injustice. My father, a refined and kindly gentleman who only hit me twice in his life, used to cuff our harmless slave boy. Lewis seemed not to resent it. It made me sorry for the victim and ashamed for the punisher. When I was ten, I saw a man throw a lump of iron in anger at a slave. It hit his skull. He died within an hour. I knew the man had a right to kill his slave if he wanted to, and yet it seemed a pitiful thing and somehow wrong, though why it was wrong I wasn't deep enough to explain if I'd been asked to do so. Nobody in the village approved of that murder—but, of course, no one said much about it.

Q. How do you explain the gap between your feelings and your inaction?

I knew that mistreatment was wrong, but I was trained by my culture to accept slavery as part of the natural order of

The Clemens family was poor when they lived in this house in Hannibal, Missouri, but they owned a slave.

things in my little town and in the South. In Nevada and California there were no slaves, and no one had much use for them anyway. By the time I went to Hawaii, and then a few years later to Europe and Palestine, the war had been fought and the Negroes had been emancipated. I began to live in the East and, though it took some getting used to, I left behind my Missouri training. I saw that the black man was no different from the white man, except for skin color and the bad influence of training.

My daughter Jean was shocked when I said that the Virgin Mary wasn't white. I explained that not one-tenth of the people alive in her day were white and that most powerfully suggests that white was not a favorite complexion with God… There's nothing important, nothing essential, about a complexion… I mean, to me. But with the Deity it's different. He doesn't think much of white people.

Q. Did your wife and her family influence your attitude toward black people?

Marrying into the Langdon family was one of the turning points in my life. I married the most wonderful woman on earth. Wherever she was, there was Eden. Her parents were abolitionists and a part of the Underground Railroad in Elmira. At the same time, I got to know the Nook Farm Hartford Circle, through my publisher. The group included some of the leaders of the emancipation movement, such as Harriet Beecher Stowe. A few years after our marriage, Livy and I moved there.

I'd already begun to realize even before I met the Langdons that slavery was unjust. I was glad the war had put an end to it. And the Negroes I remembered from my Missouri childhood were estimable folk whom I respected. I had taken their condition as slaves for granted, but I never doubted that they were human beings worthy of respect and justice and that they had feelings and brains just like

Clara Clemens studied music when her parents took her to Vienna, Austria.

white people. And that a Negro should have the same opportunities and entitlements as a white man. What we didn't realize in the South before the war—and sometimes after—is that the Negro has feelings and a heart and a moral code and is human just like the rest of us. We weren't trained to think that way.

Q. Slavery and race are issues that inevitably crop up in your work, or some of it—*Huckleberry Finn* being an obvious example.

Well, I never intended *Huckleberry Finn* to be about race and racial attitudes. Of course, it's an important part of the book, since Jim is one of the main characters and he's a slave. But the story's about Huck, the conditions of life into which he's born, and how he grows and develops and learns about what's right and what's wrong. It's about the clash between his heart and his natural instincts, and the clash between civilized rules and the pressures of society. So the story is Huck's story, not Jim's, though Jim has a story also. But it's there only because of Huck's. Given the time and the place, Huck's story has to include slavery. And because of my own life and the development of my views, it instinctively seemed to me a valuable and powerful way to have Huck attempt to discover who he is and who he wants to be.

Q. *Pudd'nhead Wilson*—your other novel about race and slavery—is primarily set before the Civil War. It's much less widely read than *Huckleberry Finn*. Why is that so, do you think?

Because it's more intense, focused, and satirically cynical. It works less as an extended story than it does as a lethally condensed satire and exposure of the folly of black-white racial distinctions, more like the angry satire of one of my favorite writers, Jonathan Swift. Its basic premise, to quote *Gulliver's Travels*, is that the human race is "the most pernicious race of little odious Vermin that Nature ever suffered to crawl upon the Surface of the Earth." And also that society makes arbitrary rules for self-interested purposes and then trains us to believe that these rules are part of nature or God-given.

Q. Can you give an example from *Pudd'nhead Wilson*?

Since everyone knew that in the South there were very few Negroes who had no white blood and very few white people who had no Negro blood, it was decided by the white folks that no matter what you looked like—and you could look entirely white—if your blood was one-twentieth Negro you were Negro and hence a slave. So in the novel I have a boy who looks white but is black. He is exchanged by his mother, who is a slave, with the white son of her master, because she fears he'll be sold down the river and she'll never see him again. And in the end, an observer with a detective-like mind named Wilson figures out what has happened. But, even after he's recognized as white and all his advantages are restored to him, the white boy who's been brought up as a slave is a mess; and the black boy who's been brought up white is a thieving rascal, but now a black one. So the purpose of defining race in that culture was to protect property, patrimony, and power. But nobody is better or worse than anybody else because of race.

Q. Slavery was abolished in 1865. Why did you publish *Pudd'nhead Wilson* in 1894, so long after abolition... and, for that matter, *Huckleberry Finn* in 1885? It would seem as if the subject was ancient history.

It was not at all ancient history. It was very much alive.

Adventures of HUCKLEBERRY FINN.

(Tom Sawyer's Comrade.)

BY

MARK TWAIN

ILLUSTRATED.

15

HUCKLEBERRY FINN

Twain's 1885 novel became his most widely read work, partly because it is where, in Ernest Hemingway's words, "all modern American literature comes from." In 1910, the influential African-American educator Booker T. Washington praised it because of the author's "deep sympathy" for the slave Jim and his "sympathy and interest in the masses of the Negro people." During the civil rights movement in the 1960s and thereafter, the novel's frequent use of the "N-word" triggered widespread accusations that Twain was a racist and the novel unsuitable for school reading lists.

Q. *Huckleberry Finn* has become the most controversial of your books. Does that surprise you?

It started off controversial. A school in Concord, Massachusetts, banned it when it was published in 1885 as being bad for kids. But that had nothing to do with race. The school authorities believed that Tom and Huck set bad examples. They did things that bad boys did, and they talked the way uneducated boys talked. So the book was banned for moral reasons, on the assumption that good boys would become bad boys by reading it. I told them that the book

The Adventures of Huckleberry Finn was criticized for providing a bad example for children.

they really ought to watch out for and never let a young person read is the Bible. Talk about bad examples!

So *Huckleberry Finn* was too **naturalistic** for the middle-class, East Coast moral censors, too much like real life in the characters, the subject matter, and the language. They wanted it cleaned up.

Q. Were you concerned that readers might think your frequent use of such a derogatory term made the book vulgar and racist?

The people of that time and place used the word as naturally and normally as any other word. I wanted my characters to talk like real people would. I'm a realist, except when I'm not. I can and do clean up a little bit. But not to have used that word in *Huckleberry Finn* would have been a dishonest distortion of the reality, untrue to the time and place. I use it to make the humanity of Jim and the problems of slavery more credible and convincing. If you think this stuff is too strong for kids, well, you're underestimating the strength of kids and protecting them from truths that sooner or later they need to know about.

Q. How would the novel have been different if Huck and Jim hadn't missed the turnoff to the Ohio River and hadn't continued going south?

Well, there wouldn't have been a novel, or it would have been a very different one. It would have been about how whites treated blacks in free states. It would have been seen as directly about post-Civil War Reconstruction race relations. It wouldn't have sold well and I would have made even more enemies.

Q. Why did you make Huck's father such a nasty, brutal, bigoted drunk?

I wanted someone in the novel to represent the nastiest kind of low-life Southern father who shows the dark side of what ignorant proslavery redneck fatherhood was like. He shows the difference between those who found slavery a reassuring way of asserting their superiority, who allowed themselves to believe that they were worth something, even if they were penniless drunkards and thieves, because they were white and not black, and those for whom slavery was a necessary evil. The respectable citizens had slavery. They needed it, they thought. And they couldn't get rid of it. But Huck's father and his kind, who never had or could own a slave, were racist in a different way. They got pleasure out of mistreating slaves. So if Huck had a father like that, what would become of him? And what is it about Huck that allows him to escape from his father's views and develop a moral sensitivity and bravery?

Q. What is it?

Huck's training hasn't been total. He still has a conscience and a good heart.

Q. Why is the last third of the book, when Jim is imprisoned on the Phelps farm because of the misguided storytelling schemes and adventures of Tom Sawyer, so different from the rest of the novel and for many readers not right, and not as good as what comes before?

I thought it was funny and would work well. I needed an ending and couldn't think of a better one. I also meant it as a satirical coda on the failure of Reconstruction. It does show Tom at his worst and Huck reluctantly going along with him. In the end, though, it results in Jim's freedom.

Q. Yet he was already free, wasn't he?

But he didn't know it, and that makes all the difference. We could all be free, if only we knew we were.

Q. What did you mean by Huck's thought at the end that he might "light out for the Territory?"

I made Tom Sawyer and Huck Finn like me in that way. Sometimes it's funny, as in Tom's inventive schemes for getting other boys to do the work he doesn't want to do, and sometimes it's heartbreaking, like Huck's thinking that maybe he could light out for the Territory and not have to put up with so-called civilization. Civilization is rules and regulations. It takes a good deal of the fun out of life, especially for restless imaginative people who like fun and don't like being told what to do and what not to do. But so-called civilization always catches up with you.

Q. Do you have any final words of advice for the human race?

Let us endeavor so to live that when we come to die even the undertaker will be sorry.

Q. But what if the undertaker represents false values and an oppressive culture?

Then tell him to go to Hell.

GLOSSARY

apogee: The highest point of something.

apprentice: Someone who works for a period of time in return for instruction for a trade from someone of skill.

autodidact: A self-taught person.

bluff reef: A shallow sand bar with deep water below it, not too much current, and in which the sand is pretty well packed.

Calvinism: A Christian set of beliefs based on the teachings of John Calvin that stresses God's power and the moral weakness of human beings.

conduit: Route that is used as a way of sending goods and services from one place to another.

conscription: Compulsory enlistment in a service, such as the military.

determinism: The belief that all events are caused by things that happened previously, and that people have no real ability to make choices or control what happens.

egocentrism: Regarding the self or individual or even a country or group as the center of all things.

ethos: The fundamental beliefs or values of a culture.

evanescent: Lasting a very short time.

heterodox: Not conforming with accepted standards or beliefs.

iconoclast: One who criticized beliefs, practices or institutions that are widely accepted.

laconic: Using few words in speech or writing.

levee: An embankment to prevent a river from overflowing.

literati: Persons interested in literature or the arts.

maxims: Well-known phrases that express general truths about life or rules about behavior.

monotheism: The belief that there is only one God.

naturalistic: Showing people or things as they really are in art or literature.

***nom de plume*:** Literally a pen name or a name adopted by a writer.

philistinism: An attitude of smug ignorance, especially toward artistic and cultural values.

predestination: The belief that everything that will happen has already been decided by God or fate and cannot be changed.

Providence: Divine guidance or care.

pseudonym: A fictitious name, especially one used by an author.

repartee: Conversation marked by quick and witty replies.

retainer: An amount of money that you pay to someone to make sure that you will have that person's services when you need them.

robber baron: An industrialist, mostly of the nineteenth century, who acquired great wealth but is thought to have done so by unethical means.

Romantic idealism: A naive, miscalculated dream of a perfect world without factoring in the flaws that reality would bring.

satirist: A writer, artist, or other creative individual who uses humor that shows the weaknesses or bad qualities of a person, government, society, etc. in their work.

secular: Not spiritual; of or relating to the physical world and not the spiritual world.

solvency: The state of being able to pay debts.

speculation: Activity in which someone buys and sells things (such as stocks or pieces of property) in the hope of making a large profit but with the risk of a large loss.

vernacular: The language or dialect spoken by ordinary people.

vitriolic: Caustic or scathing, as in vitriolic criticism.

wind reef: Not actual reefs, these water formations are caused by the wind and look just like a bluff reef to the untrained eye.

For FURTHER INFORMATION

Books

Ayers, Alex Ayres (ed.) *The Wit and Wisdom of Mark Twain*. London, England and New York, NY: HarperCollins, 1987.

Bridgman, Robert. *Traveling in Mark Twain*. London, England and Berkeley, CA: University of California Press, 1987.

Cox, James. *Mark Twain: The Fate of Humor*. Princeton, NJ: Princeton University Press, 1966.

Dolmetsch, Carl. *Our Famous Guest, Mark Twain in Vienna*. London, England and Athens, GA: The University of Georgia Press, 1992.

Kaplan, Fred. *The Singular Mark Twain, A Biography*. London, England and New York, NY: Doubleday, 2003.

Kaplan, Justin. *Mr. Clemens and Mark Twain, A Biography*. New York, NY: Simon and Schuster, 1966.

Robinson, Forrest G. (ed.) *The Cambridge Companion to Mark Twain*. Cambridge, MA: Cambridge University Press, 1995.

Smith, Henry Nash. *Mark Twain, The Development of a Writer*. Cambridge, MA: Harvard University Press, 1962.

Websites

www.twainweb.net
The website of the Mark Twain Forum is an excellent site
for book reviews, comments, controversies, and information.
The "About Mark Twain" section contains links to other
Mark Twain sites.

www.cmgww.com/historic/twain/
The official Mark Twain website maintained by the late author's
estate offers biographical information, photos, and more.

www.twainquotes.com
This site provides online access to Twain's most quoted words.

INDEX

ABOUT *the* AUTHOR

FRED KAPLAN is a distinguished Professor Emeritus of English at Hunter College who has written several acclaimed biographies, including *The Singular Mark Twain, A Biography* and *Thomas Carlyle, A Biography*, which was nominated for the 1983 National Book Critics Circle Award and was a jury nominee for the 1984 Pulitzer Prize in biography. He earned his Ph.D from Nottingham University in the United Kingdom.

JAY MCINERNEY is an American writer and food critic who gained instant fame at the age of 24 with the best-selling *Bright Lights, Big City*. He has written several other novels and collections of short stories as well as nonfiction, and has served as wine critic for the *Wall Street Journal* and as a writer at *Town and Country Magazine*.